POLICE OFFICERS

A TO Z

Text and Photographs

Jean Johnson

Walker and Company
New York, New York

Acknowledgments:

In addition to the Charlotte, N.C. Police Department, I would like to thank the Monroe, N.C. Public Safety Department, the Union County, N.C. Sheriff's Department and the Charleston, S.C. Police Department for their help.

First published in the United States of America in 1986 by the Walker Publishing Company, Inc.

Published simultaneously in Canada by John Wiley & Sons Canada, Limited, Rexdale, Ontario.

Library of Congress Cataloging-in-Publication Data

Johnson, Jean, 1943–
    Police officers, A to Z.

    (Community helpers series)
    Summary: Each letter of the alphabet introduces a topic relating to police officers and their jobs.
    1. Police—Juvenile literature. [1. Police.
2. Alphabet] I. Title. II. Series.
HV7922.J57 1986   363.2   85-26334
ISBN: 0-8027-6614-5
        0-8027-6615-3 (reinforced)

Printed in the United States of America

10 9 8 7 6 5 4 3 2 1

Book design by Laurie McBarnette

To the police officers of
Charlotte, North Carolina,
whose support and
cooperation made this book
possible

A
Accident

This police officer is at an accident. He helps anyone who is hurt. He talks to the drivers and writes down how the accident happened. The officer also directs traffic around the wrecked cars.

B
Badge

Every police officer has a badge. Officers in uniform wear the badge on their shirt. Officers who do not wear uniforms carry the badge in their pocket or purse.

C Crime

Someone has damaged this car by painting on it. This is a crime. It is against the law to harm other people's property. The officer writes down what happened and tries to find out who did it.

D

Dispatcher

Dispatchers at the police station get our calls for help. They quickly
radio a police officer. Computers make the dispatcher's job easier.

4

E
Equipment

Police officers use this equipment to help them at work. The clipboard and pen are used to write reports about everything they do. The briefcase carries maps, traffic tickets, and reports. Officers carry a whistle to direct traffic. They use a flashlight to search dark buildings and streets. Some officers carry a night stick on their belt. They use it to protect themselves.

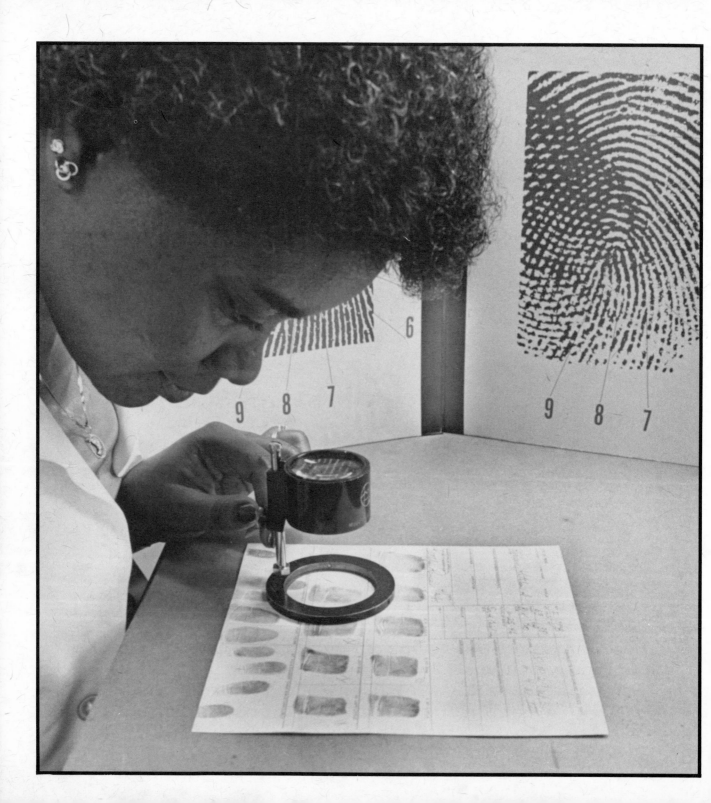

F

Fingerprints

This woman helps police officers. She works at the police station, looking at fingerprints through a magnifying glass. Everyone's fingerprints are different. Sometimes the police can tell who committed a crime by matching fingerprints.

G

Gun

Police officers carry a gun to protect themselves and the people who live in the community. Officers are very careful with their guns. Most police officers have never had to fire their guns except at target practice.

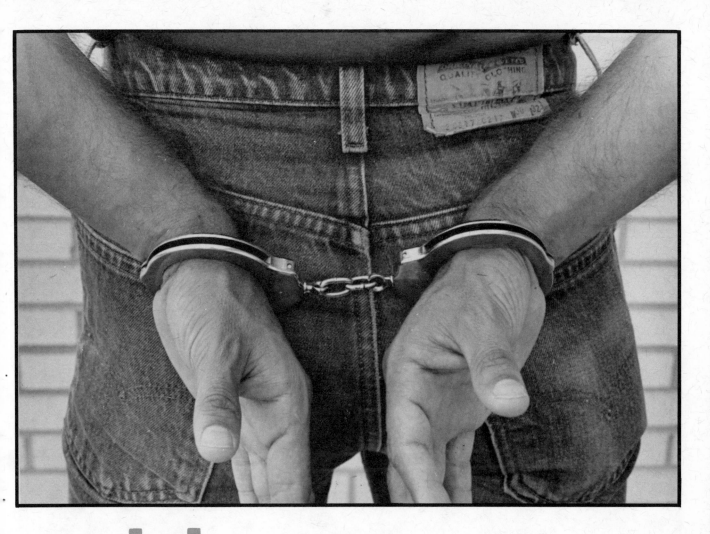

H
Handcuffs

Officers lock handcuffs on people who are arrested. This makes it hard for them to fight or get away. Police officers carry handcuffs on their belts.

Investigators

Investigators are police officers who solve crimes. They talk to people who might know something about a crime and ask them questions. Investigators look at fingerprints and search for other clues. They arrest the person they think is guilty. These officers carry guns and handcuffs, but they do not wear uniforms. Investigators are also called detectives.

J
Jail

When people are arrested, officers take them to jail. A judge decides how long a person stays in jail. The prisoner gets meals, a mattress, a blanket, and a pillow.

K
K-9

This officer and dog belong to the police K-9 unit. They are trained to work together. The dog, or canine, is taught to use his strong sense of smell and his keen ears to find people who are lost or hiding from the police. The officer controls the dog with word and hand signals.

L

Laws

Our law says you must stop at this sign. Laws are rules that make it easier for us to live together safely. Police officers make sure we obey the laws in our community.

M
Mounted
Police

Officers who ride horses are called mounted police. Horses can move in and out of traffic easily and walk on park paths or on the sidewalk. The officer can see a long way from his high seat.

N
Night

Some police officers work at night. They check stores and banks. They drive up and down the streets. They come to our homes at night if we call for help.

O
Officer

This officer has finished working for the day. He goes home to enjoy his family. He will change into regular clothes. Police officers are people just like your parents or neighbors.

P Patrol

When officers are on patrol, they watch for anything unusual or dangerous. They listen for calls from the dispatcher. Officers drive patrol cars to protect large areas and get around quickly. Patrol cars have a radio, siren, flashing light, and search light.

Some officers patrol the street on foot. They walk a beat (or area) in cities where there are a lot of people.

Quarrel

These men were quarreling and hitting each other. The police officers have helped to calm them. The officers listen to their problems and write down what happened. They want the men to use words instead of fists to settle their fight.

R

Radio

A police officer talks to the dispatcher and other officers on his car radio. The dispatcher tells him where to go to help people. The radio is very important to the officer, especially if he is in danger and needs help.

S School

This is a school for people who want to be police officers. The students learn about law and first aid. They are taught how to write reports, fire guns, and protect themselves. Students also exercise every day to make their bodies strong.

T Traffic Officer

Police officers use their hands and a whistle to direct traffic. Traffic officers tell cars when to stop and go, and they help people cross the street safely.

U

Uniform

Officers in uniform wear a shirt and pants. Equipment is carried on their belts. They wear sturdy shoes. The badge, nametag, and sleeve patch tell us who they are. They also have a raincoat for bad weather and a heavy jacket for winter.

V
Vehicles

Police officers use these vehicles as well as cars for patrolling. They all have a search light, siren, and radio. Helicopters are used to spot danger from the air and to rescue or capture people. Officers in police boats patrol the water and shore watching for accidents or for people who need help. Motorcycles are used in town and on the highway for traffic control.

W

Walkie-talkie

A walkie-talkie is a portable radio. Officers use it to talk to the dispatcher and other officers when they are not near their car radios. They use codes on the radio. Some of the codes are:

10-4	O.K.
10-17	I'm on my way.
10-30	Danger.
10-33	Help me quick.

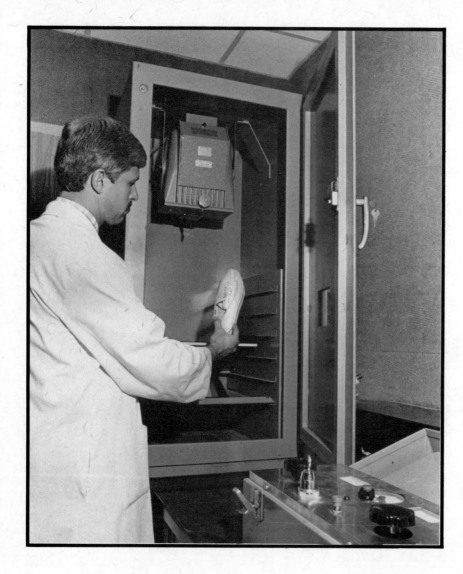

X

X-ray

This man helps the police. He uses an X-ray machine to take pictures of what's inside an object. This shoe was X-rayed to find a missing ring hidden in the sole of the shoe. Hard objects show up well in X-rays.

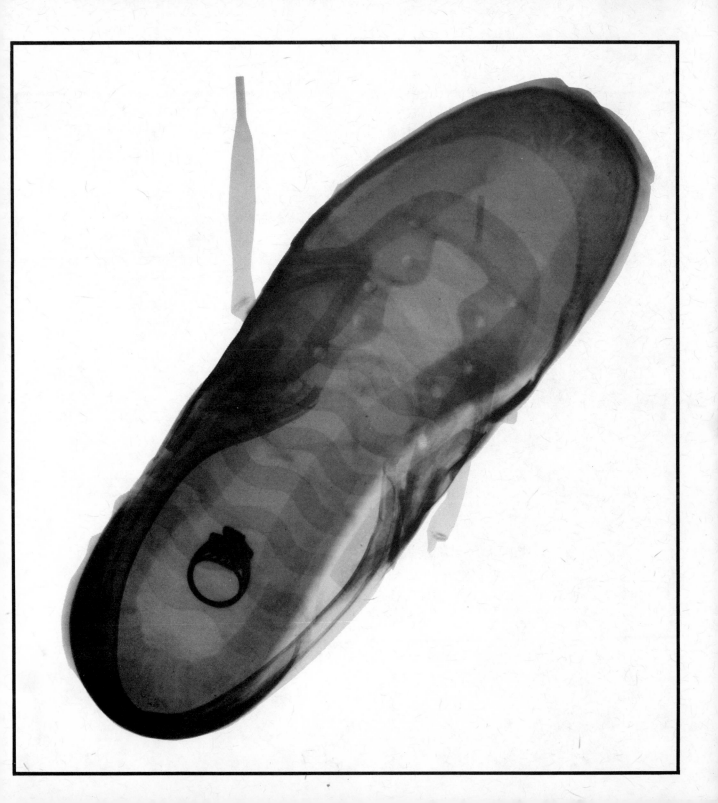

Youth Officers

Some police officers work only with children. They teach school children about safety and laws. Youth officers help children who are arrested. They talk with their parents and try to help children become better citizens.

Z
Zone Map

These officers are looking at a zone map which shows the area of the city where they work. Pins in the map show where crimes have been committed.

More About Police Officers

In this section the role of police officers is further described
in words and pictures to foster a greater awareness of the importance
of police officers in every community and to enhance classroom discussion.

Men and women who want to become police officers are carefully screened and tested before entering the police academy. They must be honest, observant, able to make quick decisions, and have good communications skills. They must care about helping people—young, old, rich, poor. They must also be willing to work day and night shifts in any kind of weather. They must be strong and healthy. They need a high school education and, in some cities, a college degree.

There are many different jobs within a police department. Patrol officers, who work alone or with a partner, make up the largest group. One of their duties is to make arrests. When an arrest is made, the officer searches the person for concealed weapons and then handcuffs him. The suspect is put into the back seat of the patrol car and taken to jail. There he is fingerprinted, photographed, and given a court date.

In addition to arrests, these officers direct traffic, issue traffic tickets for violations, and investigate crimes. Patrol officers are among the first to arrive at emergencies or disasters. They cooperate with fire fighters, rescue workers, and ambulance crews. Maintaining order at public events, such as parades and festivals, is also part of their job. Children and adults rely on police officers to answer questions and give directions.

Almost every police department has special officers who work with children. In a large city, a youth bureau may have both school resource officers and juvenile investigators. Resource officers teach classes relating to safety and law to students in kindergarten through high school. Sometimes they assist school principals with discipline problems. Juvenile investigators handle children who are missing, abused, have been victims of a crime, or who have broken the law. A juvenile is anyone under age sixteen, although this varies from state to state. Investigators use dolls to help young children talk about their problems. A young person who is arrested is usually put in a special detention center. Investigators work with social agencies to help these young people.

Other investigators might work in a vice squad, homicide, burglary or robbery details. These detectives have a desk at the police station and do much of their investigation on the telephone to save time and money. They go out to observe suspects, visit the scene of a crime, gather evidence, and make arrests. These plainclothes officers drive unmarked cars so that suspects will not know who they are. Since badges are easily duplicated, investigators carry a police identification card with them at all times.

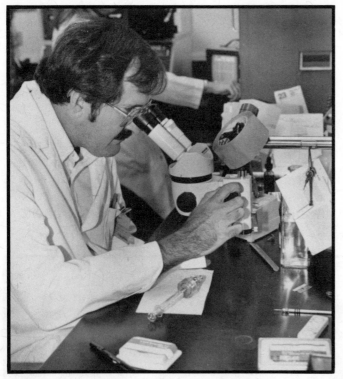

The crime lab assists police investigation by collecting and examining evidence from the scene of a crime. Using photographs, finger-prints, and samples of blood, hair, fabric or other matter, these trained individuals help solve crimes.

Many people do not realize how much paper work the police must do. Officers write reports on crimes, arrests, investigations, and other police activities. The records department keeps all these reports on file at the station. They are permanently stored in computers or on microfilm.

Television programs give a dramatic, violent view of an officer's job. Real police officers rarely use their guns and, in fact, must justify to their superiors any use of deadly force. Police departments have strict rules about using weapons and physical force. Officers who are unnecessarily aggressive are reprimanded. Many police officers act as social workers; listening to problems, calming people down, and making peace. They try to keep volatile situations under control. They are taught to restrain violent people without injuring them. Police work can be dangerous, but officers try to approach each situation intelligently.

Every community needs police officers to help and to protect its citizens. Without law enforcement, cities and towns would be chaotic and violent. Police officers make it possible for us to enjoy our families, our homes, and our jobs.

Also in the Community Helpers Series:

FIRE FIGHTERS
A TO Z